The Children's Rebellion and Climate Change

COLOURED VERSION

CHILDREN SAVING OUR PLANET SERIES

CAROL SUTTERS

Illustrated by William Fong

AuthorHouse™ UK
1663 Liberty Drive
Bloomington, IN 47403 USA
www.authorhouse.co.uk
UK TFN: 0800 0148641 (Toll Free inside the UK)
UK Local: 02036 956322 (+44 20 3695 6322 from outside the UK)

This book is printed on acid-free paper.

ISBN: 978-1-6655-8803-4 (sc)
ISBN: 978-1-6655-8804-1 (e)

Library of Congress Control Number: 2021906637

Print information available on the last page.

Published by AuthorHouse 04/26/2021

author HOUSE®

Kate and Tom are sitting watching television with their parents.

Mum cries out to the children, *"Look on the television! There is a young girl from Sweden called GRETA talking about her work to plead with adults and politicians to take action to save the planet."*

The reporter says, *"Many countries have agreed to the Paris Agreement to limit global emissions of greenhouse gases so that the rise in global temperature is below 2 degrees Celsius."*

Greta exclaims, *"The target is really to keep the rise below 1.5 degrees Celsius and we only have 7.5 years to reach this at current rate of carbon dioxide emissions. This is an EMERGENCY. Some adults do not understand that we have a climate emergency."*

The reporter continues, *"Some countries are richer than others so they will work together to help the poorer nations make changes to reduce greenhouse emissions. This is in order to defend the world from the adverse effects of climate change on ordinary people's lives."*

Greta then states, *"Technological attempts to capture carbon dioxide out of the air and planting trees will not halt the rise in climate change quickly enough. We need to slow carbon emissions urgently. The world is at a TIPPING POINT."*

"Yes," says Tom. *"This is why the Children's Rebellion demonstrated at the Houses of Parliament and we took the day off school last year. It is good that children in other countries are also standing up to support us to save the planet. They are asking their leaders to reduce carbon emissions to reduce the effects of global warming. We were told the whole planet is connected in nature, communications and businesses. What happens in one part of the world often affects another part of the world, including the weather."*

Kate confirms, *"The Children's Rebellion has declared climate change as a global emergency like the coronavirus pandemic, but, as Greta reported, many adults are not taking climate change seriously."*

Mum asks, *"Can you remember some of the extreme events that we believe have been due to temperature changes? Or other human activity which is destroying ecosystems in the world?"*

Kate answers, *"Yes, THE FLOODS. Our teacher at school, Mrs Khan, taught us that in the UK there have been many more cases of flooding in recent years. Whole towns have lost their homes and businesses. They think this could have been due to more extreme weather and temperature rises not only on land but also from Atlantic storms."*

"The floods could also have been from waterways being polluted by rubbish, destroying natural ecosystems and preventing drainage. Recently in Asia there were changes in monsoon patterns causing extreme flooding."

Tom remarks, *"Yes, Mrs Khan also said sometimes floods have happened because too many trees were cut down. This could be due to illegal logging or land clearance for mining and cattle ranching."*

Kate shouts, *"THE FIRES!"* "Yes," replies mum, *"We discussed the fires in Brazil and Australia and how this killed the trees, plants and animals, but many humans also died. The trees are very important for producing oxygen and removing carbon dioxide. The fires are becoming more frequent and more severe. The Amazon fires were the worst for more than a decade and they affected the weather in distant parts of the world."*

Tom continues, *"THE WILDLIFE. Things were different during lockdown. We used less transport and made less pollution and stayed indoors. The wildlife returned to the bogs, the birds to the trees, many more butterflies, bees and other animals were seen. Rare animals reappeared in the UK. But there were some winners and losers. Green winged orchids flourished but Ash trees became more susceptible to die back. This gave scientists a rare opportunity to see how human activity affects wildlife. Also to plan how we can all try to share space on this crowded planet in future."*

"THE FOG," says Kate. "People in some cities like Delhi, Beijing and Mumbai have a constant cloud of pollution above them which can make them ill. When they reduced the carbon they burnt during Covid 19 the sky above these cities became clear again." Mum confirms, "Yes, and it helped all those people in these cities who have respiratory diseases to breathe more easily."

Kate goes on, "THE BREAKING UP OF ICE SHEETS IN THE ANTARCTIC. We learned that warm currents are causing the ice sheets to break up and this will affect global currents, weather and the precious animals that live there. Also, we have seen summer green algae there, which darkens the snow so that it absorbs more heat and melts faster. As the ice sheets melt, coastal towns could be flooded."

Tom states, "*THE BLEACHING OF CORALS. Corals are tiny gelatinous animals that build up reefs which act as crucial marine ecosystems. We learned that the warmer temperature is causing the loss of valuable and beautiful coloured coral reef ecosystems. About half the corals have been lost in the last 30 years. Loss of coral reefs could damage coastal areas with loss of homes, work and lives.*"

Mum informs him, "*We know temperatures are due to rise. Scientists in north east Australia are in a desperate hurry to try to cross-breed corals. This will make them hardier and less easily damaged and to re-populate already damaged corals.*"

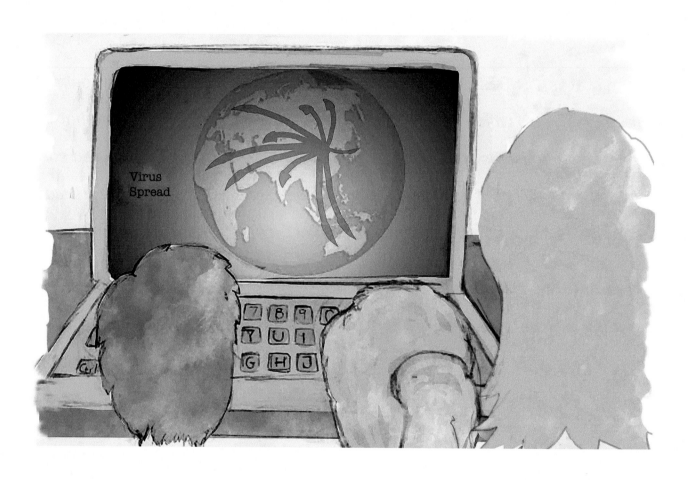

Mum reminds them, *"Let's not forget the important CORONAVIRUS worldwide epidemic. Since we invaded natural habitats and took over land for farming or industrial use, some harmful viruses have escaped their natural ecosystems. They have jumped species to infect humans and cause disease."*

"Finally, it is considered that humans have already exploited the surface of the earth for our own gain and profit. This has led to rising carbon emissions and destruction of species and habitats. The ocean depths and sea bed remain largely unexploited. We should not rush to dig up the ocean beds to release rare metal like cobalt, zinc and lithium for electric batteries, mobile phones or computers. This exploration will cause us to dump unwanted sediment rich in bacteria, with locked up carbon from millions of years ago, out into the deep seas. The sea bed is connected with surface layers and the air and this will unleash more carbon into the air."

"It will be up to young people to innovate new carbon free technologies which do not cause further destruction of the living earth."

What did we learn from today? (tick the box if you understood and agree)

☐ It is very important that we recognise the importance of what scientists say for human survival and how science can help us prevent destruction and save planet earth.

☐ Covid 19 gave us a new chance to remember a greener world, cleaner air, lower carbon emissions and so create better conditions for wildlife.

☐ We should carefully choose what we EAT, how we TRAVEL and how we LIVE to save our planet.

☐ Children should understand these science facts and work now to encourage adults and international leaders to make positive changes to save planet Earth.

☐ People are already dying from effects of climate change. This is an EMERGENCY and countries must act NOW.

☐ We should listen to advice from scientists to save the planet, to BUILD BACK BETTER and preserve our earth after Covid 19.

Children Saving our Planet Series

Books

1. **Tom and Kate Go to Westminster**

2. **Kate and Tom Learn About Fossil Fuels**

3. **Tom and Kate Chose Green Carbon**

4. **Tress and Deforestation**

5. **Our Neighbourhood Houses**

6. **Our Neighbourhood Roads**

7. **Shopping at the Farm Shop**

8. **Travelling to a Holiday by the Sea**

9. **Picnic at the Seaside on Holiday**

These series of simple books explain the landmark importance of Children's participation in the Extinction rebellion protest. Children actively want to encourage and support adults to urgently tackle both the Climate and the Biodiversity emergencies. The booklets enable children at an early age to understand some of the scientific principles that are affecting the destruction of the planet. If global political and economic systems fail to address the climate emergency, the responsibility will rest upon children to save the Planet for themselves.

This series is dedicated to

Theodore, Aria and Ophelia.

Printed in the United States
by Baker & Taylor Publisher Services